Seven Days of Change
(A Flash Devotional)

Adrienne Thompson

Pink Cashmere Publishing, LLC
Arkansas, USA

Cover design by Adrienne Thompson
Cover photo by Dave Meier via **http://picography.co**

ISBN: 0-9971461-2-5

ISBN-13: 978-0-9971461-2-7

Also by Adrienne Thompson:

Devotional:
Seven Days of Change

Anthologies:
Just Between Us (Inspiring Stories by Women) – as a contributor
The Ex Chronicles – as a contributor

Novels:
The *Bluesday* Series:
Bluesday
Lovely Blues
Blues In The Key Of B
Locked out of Heaven

The *Been So Long* Series:
Rapture
If
Been So Long
Little Sister
Been So Long 2
Been So Long III
September

The *Your Love Is King* Series:
Your Love Is King
Better

The *Ain't Nobody* Series:
Sedução (Seduction)
Ain't Nobody

The *Latter Rain* Series:
After the Pain
No Pain, No Gain
Joy and Pain

Stand-alone Novels:
See Me
When You've Been Blessed (Feels Like Heaven)
Home
Summertime

Poetry
Poetry from the Soul... for the Soul: Volume II

Introduction

Fear has always been a huge stronghold in my life and, every once in a while, it still rears its ugly head in an attempt to stop me from fulfilling what God has charged me with accomplishing. One of my greatest fears has been the fear of change. The mere thought of change, for me, has always been frightening. I experienced a lot of instability during my childhood due to my parents' divorce, and the memory of that time is not pleasant for me. So, for me, with the thought of change comes feelings of discomfort. And, like most people, I do not like being uncomfortable. I don't like it at all.

What I've learned from God is that there is often a blessing in being uncomfortable. As a matter of fact, the most wonderful blessings are often found beyond your comfort zone. Often, we fight change when God is merely trying to position us for a miracle or, at the very least, a blessing.

My prayer for you is that as you read this devotional, you seek God's will like you never have before, and you learn to embrace and celebrate the changes in your life. I encourage you to write down your thoughts, or whatever revelations the Holy Spirit plants in your heart as you read this devotional. He may reveal some life-changing revelations to you!

Finally, this is not an attempt to replace your Bible or to reinvent the wheel, it is merely me sharing with you some insights that have changed my life. I praise God for the opportunity to share them with you!!

"Come and listen, all you who fear God, and I will tell you what He did for me."
Psalm 66:16 NLT

Day 1
Praying and Staying

For years, I attended a great church that I was led to in the midst of some of the deepest sorrow and turmoil I've ever experienced. I am of the belief that every pastor has a niche. This pastor's niche was encouragement, and Lord knows I needed plenty of that.

I grew in spiritual maturity while attending that church. I began to read the Bible, and a hunger for more spiritual knowledge grew so great inside of me that I found myself doing online Bible studies and attending Christian groups outside of my church. I needed more. I needed to delve deeper into my faith, and one day, a reality hit me. What I was seeking could not be found at my church. God was almost audibly telling me that I had gotten what I needed there, and it was time to move on. I didn't understand this. I loved my church home. This was not something I was comfortable with doing. So I decided to pray about it. Looking back, that decision seems rather silly. Why would I need to pray about something God, Himself, was telling me to do? My guess is that I was really praying that He'd change His mind, so I wouldn't have to do something that felt uncomfortable.

I was stubborn. While "praying" I stayed put, attending church every Sunday. Well, there was no peace in my praying and staying. My mind was in such turmoil that I couldn't even concentrate on the sermons. It was like I was just sitting there, passing time and getting nothing out of the services. So, I stopped praying, and I moved on. After a short search, I settled into a new church home where I found just what I had been craving. It was not the same denomination. It was not full of the tradition my past church homes were steeped in. But it was what I needed, when I needed it.

I shared this because someone is holding onto tradition. Someone is being loyal to a pastor or a building when their loyalties should be with God. Someone is afraid to be uncomfortable, and they are missing a deeper revelation and a bigger experience. Someone is praying and staying. Stop praying for Him to change His mind and change *yours*.

Maybe you have not experienced what I described. Maybe

there are other areas of your life where God is prompting you to make a change or to make a move. Whatever the case, choose not to use prayer as a cop-out as we often do. Instead of praying and staying, choose obedience, and *move your feet.*

Today's Scripture:
"But Samuel replied: 'Does the LORD delight in burnt offerings and sacrifices as much as in obeying the LORD? To obey is better than sacrifice, and to heed is better than the fat of rams.'"
1 Samuel 15:22 NIV

Notes

Day 2

Make That Move

In December of 2010, I was met with a unique and daunting opportunity. A former supervisor had an opening for a nurse in Conway, Arkansas. I was living in Pine Bluff, Arkansas at the time. I'd never even been to Conway, and in my mind, it was a thousand miles away instead of the 70 or so miles that actually separated it from Pine Bluff.

My first response was an emphatic "no." I didn't even know where Conway was! Most of my family, and all of my friends, were in Pine Bluff. Why on earth would I move away from the town I'd called home since I was three years old? What kind of sense did that make? I had it good in Pine Bluff. I had a good job, and I was living rent-free in a home owned by my family. Sure, it wasn't in the best of neighborhoods, and neglect (some on my part and some caused by other family members who shared the home) had made living conditions less than desirable, but still, I had a good life in my home town, didn't I?

After I ended that conversation with my former supervisor, I shook my head at the thought of taking her up on her offer. It just seemed like pure insanity to me. Honestly, the thought of moving to, and living in, another town and taking my young daughter out of school in the middle of the year had never crossed my mind before, and I didn't think it ever would. But then, God spoke to me.

As clear as day, I heard Him say, "*Why not move?*"

Huh? Really? Was He serious? Why *not* move*?* Well, I had a list of reasons *why not*. Didn't He hear my thoughts? Didn't He know why not?

Why not move?

Three little words. Three little words that would not leave my mind. Three little words that would, eventually, change my life.

Those words danced around in my head for days. And then I fell into the same trap again—I decided to pray about it. I prayed and prayed and prayed, and waited and waited and waited. See a pattern here? And then I decided to seek the counsel of a friend. What she had to say blew my mind.

"You should go. I think life will be better for you if you move. I've always seen you with a dark cloud hanging over your head, and I think it will be lifted if you move. It's nice to be near family, but you need to leave and find your own way."

I was shocked, to say the least. I wasn't sure how to take what she'd said. I was close to my family members. How would they take the news? How would my daughter feel about moving and changing schools in the middle of the year? What would I do with no friends in a new place? I was a home health nurse. How would I navigate this new territory?

So I continued to pray and stay. What did I say before? Right! There's no peace in praying and staying. So I asked my young daughter how she felt about moving. I hated to even bring it up since several instances of bullying had prompted me to move her to a private school that fall. This move would mean she'd be changing schools for the third time in less than a year. As expected, she was upset… for exactly three minutes. Then she decided she really didn't mind at all. She actually thought it would be fun, an adventure. And to be honest, since she was the only person really being affected by the move other than me, her opinion was the only one that counted. So I moved forward, having waited so long that I missed the window of opportunity to simply transfer into the new position. I had to apply and interview like a complete stranger.

I did just that. And, knowing that God was in this plan, I went ahead and found a place to stay without confirmation that the job was mine. But then again, I did have confirmation, didn't I? My confirmation came the moment God said, "*Why not move?*"

I got the job, and on December 30, 2010, I moved away from the only place I'd ever called home with very little furniture, hardly any money in the bank, and a preteen daughter in tow. My future was uncertain. I was very afraid. But God is faithful. That move was one of the best decisions I've ever made in my *entire life*. It has been a blessing for both me and my daughter. Had it not been for that move, I never would have published even one book, because of the environment and the mentality I was stuck in (I'll elaborate on that more later on).

What about you? Has God prompted you to make a move or take a leap of faith, but fear and uncertainty have paralyzed you? Take a moment and fully realize that if God calls you to

move, He already knows how everything will work out, and it WILL be to your advantage.

Today's Scripture:
"The LORD had said to Abram, 'Go from your country, your people and your father's household to the land I will show you.'"
Genesis 12:1 NIV

Notes

Day 3
A Change in Order

I'd just joined a new church that had all of the things I wanted and needed in a church experience—great teaching and preaching, great fellowship, an awesome choir, and a very strong youth department. I was in awe of this place, and I LOVED being there. I tried my best to spend as much time there as I possibly could. I rarely missed a Sunday, and I attended many of the different events held throughout the week—Bible studies, praise services, concerts.

I had no complaints at all. It was almost too good to be true that I was being fed in such a wonderful environment. I was so happy and so determined to grow in God; for the first time in my life, I decided to attend Sunday School.

For those who don't know, Sunday School is held early on Sunday mornings, before the weekly worship service. In Sunday School, you learn more about God and the Bible. This church had several options for specialized Sunday School classes, including a class designed for, and led by, women. A friend, who was a long-time member of the church, invited me to the women's class, and I readily accepted. I walked into class that Sunday morning with a heart full of expectation. What I got was not what I bargained for.

We were assigned a book to read and were to discuss parts of it during Sunday School. At least that was the class's agenda. However, the class leader had her *own* agenda, and it had nothing to do with that book or the lessons therein.

Her agenda was to preach or discuss any and every thing other than what was in that book, or at least that's how it seemed to me. Instead of attending a Sunday School class, I felt more like I was sitting in the audience during the taping of a Christian talk show. This would've been fine, but the lessons in the book were actually really good and more than worth discussing. What she was doing was out of order, and it disturbed me, because my God is definitely a God of order.

At first, I thought I was being too rigid. After all, they *were* praying and preaching. Maybe I was just thinking too much or reading too much into what was going own. Maybe I was being a little legalistic. Lord knows I didn't want that to be the case.

I bet by now you've already guessed what I did. Yep, I stayed. I stayed in hopes of things getting better. Guess what? They didn't. And so, I decided to pick another class. Once I stopped attending the women's class, I got some odd looks from the women who were still in that class. The leader even gave me some looks. But, let me tell you, the new class blessed my soul! I learned so much and was even able to get plugged into a ministry and through that class, began to serve.

We should never be afraid to step away from something and make a change just because what is going on seems to be Godly when it is actually out of order with what SHOULD be going on. God is a God of order. Now, of course, order should never quench the Holy Spirit, but remember, the Holy Spirit is a Spirit of order and purpose, as well.

Today's Scripture:
"For God is not a God of disorder but of peace—as in all the congregations of the Lord's people."
1 Corinthians 14:33 NIV

Notes

Day 4

More Money, More Problems

I got married at the age of sixteen to the father of the child I bore at fifteen. We were young and in love and, at the time, that was all that mattered to us. We weren't concerned about practical things like money or jobs or a home. We just wanted to be together.

We struggled financially *and* mentally. We had to live with relatives. We were on public assistance, and lacking became a way of life. I became an expert at making payment arrangements with the bill collectors. I could stretch a buck like no other to feed myself and my family. I knew the cheapest brands of everything. I had clutched onto survival mode and was holding on for dear life.

As the years passed, my marriage fell apart, and I found myself single with three children to raise, a small amount of child support, and an education but no job. I went back to school, became an RN, and started making decent money. Things were changing for me and my family, but I still had a firm grip on survival mode. I was still in the mindset that I didn't have enough, and with that mindset comes sacrifices. For instance, if you are barely scraping by, you're not going to run to the auto mechanic just because the air conditioning in your car goes out; you simply roll the windows down. If your washer goes on the blink, you start going to the Laundromat. If your stove stops working, you buy a hot plate. In survival mode, there is no such thing as saving money for the repairs. There *is* no money to save. All there is is just enough to scrape by, just enough for the end of one month to meet the beginning of the next. A savings account is a joke in survival mode.

Herein lies the problem: I had the money! Remember, I had a good job as an RN. All I had to do was save it and get the repairs done. But in my mind, I convinced myself that it was impossible. In my mind, it was better to spend the money on the hot plate or fast food or the Laundromat. It made more sense to me, because the money had never been there before, so it couldn't be there now… could it? That experience taught me just how powerful our minds are. I learned that if you are stuck in a certain mindset, it can shape your world. My world was shaped in the mindset that I could not do better now, because I couldn't do better in the past, and what that mindset got me was a house full of broken stuff. By thinking I didn't have enough, I ended up living in a way that was far below what God wanted for me and I wanted for myself. But worst of all, my children had to live through that.

Essentially, what I did was waste my money trying to put Band-Aids on problems that required major surgery, because my mind had convinced me that the surgery was beyond my reach. In order to change my life, I had to change my thinking. In order to live in a manner pleasing to God, I had to realize that His desire for me was not to merely survive, but to thrive. I had the money at my disposal, I just had to use it in the right way.

Part of the problem was my environment. Moving, as discussed in a previous chapter, helped reshape my mindset. Leaving the "broken stuff" behind made all the difference in the world.

Has this ever happened to you? Have you been so accustomed to one way of living that you totally ignored the fact that better was within your reach (this can pertain to relationships, jobs, etc.)? If so, open your eyes and see the things God wants for you, and then begin to want them for yourself. Know that He will always take care of your true needs.

Today's Scripture:
"...My purpose is to give them a rich and satisfying life."
John 10:10 NLT

Notes

Day 5
Start Wanting What You Need and Stop Needing What You Want

In November of 2012, I made a decision that changed my life and rocked my world. I decided to leave a career that had afforded me a good life, a decent salary, and great benefits. My career had been a necessity for a long time, and it had enabled me to take care of my three children as a single mother. But as good as my job had been to me in some ways, it had been equally bad to me in other ways, leaving me feeling overworked, stressed out, and just plain unhappy.

In 2012, I published four books and watched my monthly book income rise. I saved the money, and after reflecting on the modest success of my book career, wondered if I would one day be able to quit my job and pursue writing full-time. It was a stretch. I mean, I hadn't saved *that* much money. I wasn't making *that* much money from books, either. But it was a thought that wouldn't leave my mind. The mere possibility of being free from my job, of being my own boss, was so exciting! It would mean freedom, *real* freedom.

So this time I prayed... *and* I listened. And God directed me to quit my job with the reassurance that He wouldn't let me fail. And then there was the thought in the back of my head that if I did fail, I could always fall back on my nursing license. There was always the possibility of getting another nursing job if I just had to.

I made plans to quit in January of 2013. That way I could save up even more money.

God said, "*Quit now.*"

So in November, I turned in my two-week notice and left the security of my nine to five for the uncertainty of self-employment. I felt happy, relieved, and petrified. Though God had already reassured me that I would not fail or fall, I was anxious about my ability to take care of my daughter without my sure-thing nursing job. As stressful as it was, and as unhappy as I was in it, it had come to be my "source" in my mind—not God. Well, God cleared that up really quickly for me.

Month after month, He showed me the truth. HE was, still is, *and always will be* my source. Yes, some months were tighter than others. And yes, I had to make sacrifices. But let me tell you, I'd rather give up a DVR or satellite radio (that I wasn't even listening to) than the peace of mind and lowered stress level that came along with quitting my job.

I have learned so much during this period of my life—much more than I bargained for. I've learned that some of the things in my life that I thought I needed, I really didn't need at all. Our society has turned some of the things that are wants into needs. I don't *need* every channel on the cable roster. I don't *need* to buy a new purse every month. I don't *need* to eat out every time I feel like it. All I really need is food, shelter, clothes, and love—and I have those things in abundance. God has made sure of that.

What this experience has taught me is that I prefer the freedom of being my own boss. I prefer having more time to spend with my daughter. I prefer not being so tired and dragged out that I cannot cook or clean. I prefer lowered blood pressure. I prefer being able to stay in bed when I am sick without threat of penalty from my job. I prefer these things so much that I'm willing to give up some of the things I once thought I had to have. What was once so important to me, is no longer important at all, because I have tasted this life of freedom, and I'm not willing to let it go.

Are there things in your life that you think you can't live without? Why don't you take this challenge: do without them for a week, whether they be a TV show or a visit to your favorite coffee shop? Instead of focusing on these things, focus on spending more time with your family or, most importantly, with God. You may find that life is sweeter when you let some things go. And you might gain more than you anticipated.

Today's Scripture:
"And my God will meet all your needs according to the riches of His glory in Christ Jesus."
Philippians 4:19 NIV

Notes

Day 6

At Least

I can remember for years having a desire to be rich and famous—one way or the other. I read all of the entertainment magazines, watched the gossip shows and awards shows religiously. If there was a star I liked, I learned all I could about them. I wanted to know what they did to get where they were. I studied them, studied their lives, and tried to learn the skills that were behind becoming successful.

I loved all things Hollywood, I loved books, and I loved all types of music. But I was taught early on that a proper life included a proper education and a proper career. My parents were both very scholarly and very successful in their careers—groundbreaking, even. So after a few bumps in the road, I ended up on the course that everyone approved of. I enrolled in college and excelled in many subjects, never really mastering or enjoying any of them except for English. English had always been a strong suit for me. Writing, and writing well, had always come easily. I wrote poetry to express my feelings when my shyness wouldn't allow me to verbalize them. But writing was not an acceptable career. No one actually told me that, but I knew it wasn't on the list of careers I'd been told *were* acceptable. And to be honest, I never even thought about pursuing an artistic career. Careers like that are for stars. I wasn't a star, and I never would be.

So I pursued and earned a degree in Biology pretty easily. Next was Medical School. I took the MCAT (Medical College Admission Test) and did fairly well—well enough to be considered for conditional admission. My highest score was on the writing portion. Actually, my writing score was *excellent*. But I just couldn't do it. Medical school wasn't a good fit for me, and nothing felt right about pursuing a career in medicine. *Nothing.* I had two small children and a husband at the time, and I couldn't see sacrificing my family (because that's what would have been required of me, in essence) to pursue something that was not in my heart.

I went on to work different jobs before getting divorced and being forced to find a way to take care of my children. I needed a specialized degree of some sort that would ensure me the security of a good job with good pay. I opted to enter a 28-month nursing program. And after successfully completing the coursework, became an RN.

Was my heart in nursing? No. But my head was in the fact that I had three mouths to feed, no husband, and a small amount of child support.

I went on to work several nursing jobs, seeking a fit that would never be found, because nursing was not my calling. Nursing was not what made my heart leap. It was still the entertainment world and stories and books and music that got my blood running and made my mind race.

There's only so long a person can live without pursuing their passion. Or maybe I should say that living without pursuing your passion is not really living at all. It is, more or less, just existing. In 2009, I was fed up with existing. I was tired of carrying around the "at least I have a job" mentality that so many of us hold as a sad, defeating mantra. To me, that is an insult to God. To me, that's like saying that God is the god of "at least" instead of the god of "immeasurably more than we can ask or think…" *(Ephesians 3:20 NIV)*. I was convinced that there was more for me than five o'clock and payday. There *had* to be more! And so I prayed and asked God what my "more" was.

First, He reminded me that I could write and that I was rather good at it. Then He showed me all of the things I'd been through— the good and the bad, happiness and heartbreak, struggle and triumph. He showed them to me, told me they were not to be wasted; they were to be shared. And then… and then the Creator of the universe, the Almighty God, began to pour story after story into my mind. And I began to write them. And I found my calling. I found my purpose. I found a life beyond "at least."

All of that research, all of those desires, all of that talent, a desire to reach beyond the normal—He put it there for a reason. He put it there that He might use it for His glory.

Is there something you ache to do that is against the norm? Is there a dream that resides inside of you that is so big, you're not even sure it makes sense? Well, it does! God didn't place those dreams and aspirations inside of you for no reason! There is a divine reason for everything. And if God put it inside of you, He will bring it out if you just trust Him enough to try. Do not

worry about what others say or think about you pursuing your dream. Of course it won't make sense to them. It's not their dream! Trust God, and watch Him make the naysayers your biggest fans.

And remember, this applies to more than just dreams. I've heard people in bad and/or abusive relationships say, "At least I have a man," or "At least I'm not alone." "At least" has no place in a Christian's vocabulary. Commit to living a life that consists of more than "at least."

Today's Scripture:
"Now to Him who is able to do immeasurably more than all we ask or imagine, according to His power that is at work within us…"
Ephesians 3:20 NIV

Notes

Day 7
Weaknesses and Limitations

I am overweight. Medically, I am morbidly obese. I have been overweight for several years due to a stressful childhood and years of vying with anxiety and depression. I have not been thin since I was in the second grade. I have accepted the fact that I will probably never be thin in the world's sense of the word. But I am ambling along the road to becoming more fit. I am fighting the fight to become healthier, and yes, I am trying to lose weight.

This has been nearly a lifelong struggle for me. It has been hard, and for a long time, I packaged my self-worth in my appearance. I decided there was no way I deserved good things if I looked the way I looked. I didn't really love or respect myself or my body, and in turn, I didn't expect anyone else to respect me or my body. I let people run over me. I gave myself away sexually at an early age. I allowed these things, because I truly thought I didn't deserve any better and that the only way to keep people in my life was to give them something—my self-respect, my body, my peace, *anything*.

In my mind, there was just no way for me to do the things I desired to do or live the life I wanted to live in my condition, *in this body*.

This carried on into my writing career. As I wrote story after story, I lived in fear of sharing my work. I actually wondered how I could be an author at my size. I was sure people wouldn't accept me or my work. It seems silly to me now, but that was really how I felt. To me, obesity was a king-sized limitation. I was just too big to be happy... or successful.

But then there were times when I didn't see myself that way. There were times when I looked in the mirror and saw myself as a beautiful woman, deserving of happiness. Those were the times when I was at my absolute best—confident and unstoppable. And while I was reveling in self-love, Satan was making plans to pull me back down into the pit of self-despair. Like clockwork, he would place someone in my path who would remind me that I was a fat girl—nothing more, nothing less. And soon, I'd find myself back at square one, and what I saw in the mirror was no longer beautiful to me. My poor self-image was a HUGE weakness for me. But what had slipped my mind was that where I was weak, God was strong.

When I finally decided to pursue this writing dream, I found that people not only accepted my work, they *readily* accepted it and enjoyed it. And for the first time, I realized that my weight was largely a limitation in my mind. I had made it a handicap, and instead of working to change it, I'd settled into my role of being unhappy.

What about you? Is there something you believe is holding you back? Take a good long look in the mirror, and do what I learned to do—see yourself as God sees you. No matter your size, race, age, or disability, God can use you... if you let Him.

Today's Scripture:
"But He said to me, 'My grace is sufficient for you, for my power is made perfect in weakness.' Therefore I will boast all the more gladly about my weaknesses, so that Christ's power may rest on me."
2 Corinthians 12:9 NIV

Notes

_____

_____

_____

_____

_____

_____

_____

_____

_____

_____

_____

_____

_____

_____

_____

_____

_____

_____

_____

_____

_____

_____

_____

Thank you so much for reading this devotional. It is my prayer that the words on these pages have blessed you in some way. God bless you in all that you do!

~Adrienne Thompson

Online Bible:
https://www.biblegateway.com/

To learn more about Author Adrienne Thompson, visit,
http://adriennethompsonwrites.webs.com

You can email Adrienne directly at **tapestrywriter@gmail.com**

Sign up for Adrienne's newsletter here: **http://eepurl.com/jnDmH**

Follow Adrienne on Twitter!
https://twitter.com/A_H_Thompson

Like Adrienne on Facebook!
https://www.facebook.com/AdrienneThompsonWrites

Follow Adrienne on Pinterest!
http://www.pinterest.com/ahthompsn/

www.ingramcontent.com/pod-product-compliance
Lightning Source LLC
Chambersburg PA
CBHW061758040426
42447CB00011B/2371